Yearnings

poems by

Stephanie Harper

Finishing Line Press
Georgetown, Kentucky

Yearnings

Copyright © 2025 by Stephanie Harper
ISBN 979-8-89990-105-8 First Edition
All rights reserved under International and Pan-American Copyright Conventions. No part of this book may be reproduced in any manner whatsoever without written permission from the publisher, except in the case of brief quotations embodied in critical articles and reviews.

ACKNOWLEDGMENTS

The following poems were previously published in the below listed publications:

Tupelo Press' *30/30 Project*: Snapshot; Midwinter; Fragments; Gifts; Excarnation
Midwest Literary Magazine, February 2011: Dawn
Poetry Quarterly, Fall 2010: Sonnet at a Starbucks

Publisher: Leah Huete de Maines
Editor: Christen Kincaid
Cover Art: Stephanie Harper
Author Photo: Kyle Colby, KColby Photography
Cover Design: Elizabeth Maines McCleavy

Order online: www.finishinglinepress.com
also available on amazon.com

Author inquiries and mail orders:
Finishing Line Press
PO Box 1626
Georgetown, Kentucky 40324
USA

Contents

Human	1
Lombard Street	2
Conversation	3
Snapshot	4
You and I	5
Oceans	6
Sonnet at a Starbucks	7
Cellular	8
Windows	9
The Unexplored	10
What it Looks Like	11
Spit and Mud	12
Touch	13
Magic and Miracles	14
Midwinter	15
Handshake	16
Fragments	17
Gift	18
Excarnation	19
Reaching	20
Special K	21
Sunset	22
Dawn	23
Love with Skin On	24

To the ones who taught me what it is to love, to lose, to long for.

Human

Night travels
in waves
of crossfire.

Wings beat
soundless
in the chambers of

your smile.
The undertone
of a second guessing,

the flash in your eyes,
reminds me that
you are human.

Lombard Street

"Crookedest street in all of San Fran," he says,
turning the wheel like a fifteen-year-old boy
on an arcade machine, loose change in pocket,
as the excitement of driving like some kind of stud,
a Bond or McQueen,
makes him squeal and push down on the pedal.

But I don't really notice him.

I'm sitting in the backseat of the van,
as it careens like a runaway train,
distracted by the unassuming action of your fingers on my knee,
an innocent affection,
igniting sensations that twist my insides,
the same bends that cause me to fall against you—

jelly in the backseat of a momentary death machine.

Conversation

Hours drift between words and

I can sink or swim
in subtle traces,
dive beyond undercurrents,
letters strung together,

the ones that escape your mouth.

I intuit wavelengths
as you emit them,
and curls of smoke intone
who you are.

Your secret is safe with me.

Snapshot

This love exists
in subsurface mysteries

unnoticed in boxes
of old photographs

where cast-iron eyes
anticipate sunlight.

You and I

You breathe
with quiet songs
of mess and waste and

I cannot always taste it.
I have only begun to
understand

the mystery of those moments,
the secrets you keep
in the center of your chest.

Oceans

You are somewhere
miles away

and I wish you were here,
because you use words
like a weapon,

and while this cuts like glass
on other days,

tonight it's a remedy
for the ideas in my head.

Sonnet at a Starbucks

Do I smell the stale coffee on your breath?
Can I taste the smoke of your cigarettes?
It's always hard to say. You know the rest.
A penny I pay you, always in debt.

I hear rumors in your crackling skin.
I touch the dark, imagine how I would
lace each finger of your hand in my hand.
Tell me, do I give everything I can?

Does the excitement curl from your chest
like steam as it bubbles through city streets?
Or do I imagine? Your eyes express
everything and nothing: rinse and repeat.

I see you now as though it were the first,
the last, the fair, the faint, and unrehearsed.

Cellular

Your words amble and
I misapprehend when

I cannot see your face or
know what you are thinking.

I search for meaning
in fragments and

melt in the hollow
of your voice in my head.

Windows

My eyes are glassy,
guilty with windows
too fogged over
with shame,
with regret,
with every word unspoken and
clinging to the panels
like mold.

But you—
may you be the rock
that crashes through
and in the chards,
the brokenness,
may our light shine.

The Unexplored

I've seen worlds of subsurface
desire boil through the cracks
in the dirt on your back.

I've sponged every ounce
of laughter from the open halls
in the hollow of your chest.

I've tasted salt where tears
have dripped through the ivy
winding its way around your waist.

I've bathed in oceans
in the salty whispers of
the tangles of your hair.

I've trailed secret passageways
hidden against the folds of the
corners that connect your limbs.

I've heard sighs as they echoed
in the cavernous space between
the touching of our lips.

I've felt you move inside me
when I'm covered in the
island of your body.

I've explored each unlocked
door—parts of you—and still
there's more to know.

What It Looks Like

Even when my throat is dry
with the cracked sorrow
of the same conversation
we turn over and over,
your hand holds a glass of water,
and the fingers of the other
are wrapped around my shoulder,
so I know I've seen
the secret in your smile,
the one that spreads,
tethered to my own.

Spit and Mud

My love for you is spit and mud.
It's a crude material
but it's what I've got
and that matters more

than the ingredients.

My life with you is rock and roll.
It sounds glamorous in stereo,
but it has a serrated edge
and the record is scratched

but we play it anyway.

Touch

When the time came for us,
I found it hard to undress,
afraid you'd trace
the curve of my back
and find the blemishes
I'd hidden, dark splotches
just underneath my skin.

Still, I let you unwrap me.

You reached out to touch
the bruises and it didn't hurt
the way I thought it would
when your fingers
pressed against me.

I didn't expect
that gentleness.

Magic and Miracles

You've drawn a slender line
between your magic and your miracles.

One crackles in the damp heat
of the spaces that form
when our bodies come together—
small nooks—and the air is electric.

This is your magic.

This is your grand, fleeting hocus pocus
where you find your way inside,
flint sparking and igniting joy,
and I believe you'll know what it means
to exist there always.

Still, while I desire this conjuring
like a sunflower in the morning light,
it is a momentary gift.

Your miracles are less imposing.

They exist in patterns of daily phenomena,
the ones you turn over
in the peaceful quiet of running water,
like a warm bath, or the gentle whisper
of a summer breeze.

These miracles endure in twilight,
when the stars are
just beginning to shine.

Midwinter

You live less like a bird
with a broken wing,
or a scared animal
that waits for coaxing
with a few scraps of food,
and more with the quiet cadence
of a midwinter song.

I could learn something
from your constancy,
the steadiness of it,
slow and oft repeated,
a refrain.

Handshake

There's a certain ease
in the soft pads of your fingers
against the back of my hand,
the subtle squeeze,
bone on bone,
the flesh of my knuckles
stretched thin and taut,
a kind of recognition that this,
two open palms,
is the closest we'll ever come.

Fragments

Let's talk about fragments,
of matter,
of tiny pieces of you and I,
how they flutter and fall,
like dying leaves,
crinkled and broken,
no longer useful
to our branches.

And you walk over the mess
crackling underfoot,
sweep piles of the dead
to toss into trash bags.

Maybe these fragments
are actually skin
shedding itself to grow new,
fresh layers
to begin again.

Gift

That I'd fallen
through
the cracks
with you,
that too,
was a gift.

One I hadn't
found
the distance
to unwrap.

Excarnation

If you were to take a fileting knife,
cold and exacting,
and cut deep into my arm,
down to the bone,
with a surgical precision,
you could peel back
the layers of my skin,
every inch of my body
until I was exposed.

We excarnate the dead,
but I am still living
and if you are looking
for who I am
you only need to ask.

I'll give you the answers
with freedom.

Reaching

You pour yourself into
the broken ground,
crumbling into dust
inside me.

This mud,
you mold it
with the long bones
of your fingers
stretching out
with the anticipation
that I too
might reach out
for you.

Special K

For me, it was always you.
For you, it was never me.

Yes, we collided
like a car crash,
tires screeching and
shattered glass,
never tender,
always ravenous.

I hungered for something beyond satiety.

You hungered for something convenient:
trail mix in a ziploc bag,
easy to dispose of,
still licking the salt from your fingertips.

I cannot blame you for this.

You cannot force someone's desire.
You cannot will them into wanting you forever.

You can only find ways to fill the emptiness,
a bad stomachache,
like the cavern of your navel widens
with each breath.

Sunset

Sunlight streaks the sky
in cranberry bands
fading into the twilight.

This is the opulent final bow,
before moonlight,
before the cover of stars.

This is our cycle of hours.

Dawn

With vibrancy
you hoist
yourself
up.

Your tendrils
stroke,

with
warmth,

my unclothed skin,

stretched outward in the morning.

Love with Skin On

Love comes with skin on,
heart beating
and pumping blood.

Love is breathing,
being,
ready to take your hand.

Don't ever think
you must do this
by yourself.

Don't ever wonder
if the whole of you
is worthy.

You (yes, *you*)
are loved
are love.

Stephanie Harper is the author of the novel Wesley Yorstead Goes Outside, winner of the 2020 Next Generation Indie Book Awards, as well as a finalist for the Colorado Book Awards and the National Indie Excellence Awards. She is also the author of the poetry collection *Sermon Series,* previously published by Finishing Line Press in 2017. Her narrative nonfiction work can be found in a number of publications, including *HelloGiggles, HuffPost, Living Lutheran, Healthline,* and more. She often writes about chronic illness and spirituality.

Stephanie grew up in Colorado, where she graduated from CU Boulder with a BA in English in 2009. She received her MFA in Creative Writing from Fairfield University in 2012. She's worked on several literary magazines, including *Mason's Road* and *Spry Literary Journal.* She also served as a guest editor for *The Puritan,* where she wrote and curated pieces about narrative generosity.

Stephanie currently lives in Colorado with her family.

www.ingramcontent.com/pod-product-compliance
Lightning Source LLC
Chambersburg PA
CBHW022103080426
42734CB00009B/1479